Guide to a Richer Life

GUIDE TO A RICHER LIFE

Know Your Worth Find Your Voice Speak Your Truth

Donna Rustigian Mac

Guide to a Richer Life

Know Your Worth, Find Your Voice, Speak Your Truth

By

Donna Rustigian Mac

ISBN-13: 978-0-578-64819-4

Written by Donna Rustigian Mac

Cover design by Eva Ruutopold

Dedications

*For the many professionals I've had the
honor of supporting AND learning from.*

For Jeff

who inspires courage and confidence.

For my cherished daughters,

Alyssa and Julia,

who are building

rich, healthy lives

through effective communication

Contents

Testimony

Donna Mac has successfully bridged the gap between professional speaking and sincere interpersonal communication. As a media professional, she learned to use the power of her words to entertain and inform millions. She has also done the tough work necessary to understand the subtleties of human dynamics, in all areas of life. Perhaps most important – Donna is a great speaker and coach. She can help you have those hard conversations you've been putting off. She will empower you to live the most valuable personal and professional life possible through high-level effective communication.

Dr. Jack Casey, Media General Manager
Emerson College
Boston, Massachusetts

Foreward

Speaking our truth is seen as challenging and rig-
orous to many. Even polished and poised people,
at one point or another, choose to avoid it. Many
of us choose not to communicate in a truthful and
forthright manner because we believe it will allevi-
ate stress. We think it will help us keep some kind
of peace in our lives.

But the initial peace we're trying to achieve keeps
us from growing as individuals; is linked to immediate, fast-fleeting gratification; and can be the
basis for great distress. When our voices need to
come up and out but remain stifled, anxiety and
the sense that we are navigating this world alone
can begin to emerge.

Keeping our voices quiet instead of learning how
to communicate effectively has become an epi-
demic. Millions of people choose to text or email

rather than talk face-to-face, and worse, we often suppress, disregard, or ignore what needs to be talked about.

At this pivotal point in time, it is vital that we assess how our society is currently connecting and communicating. Notice that while technology is increasing, human interaction is waning.

If we can slow or reverse this decline, everyone will win.

As they begin their adult lives, Generations Y and Z can gain an advantage by becoming skilled and nimble in technological, business, AND communication skills alike.

Seasoned professionals can also have an advantage because communicating effectively and consistently will become a less strenuous task! By embracing some of the most challenging work there is (on earth!) we can evolve as individuals. We can become stronger and more mindful of what really is at stake.

Plus, isn't having healthy human connections what life is all about?

We could have every "thing" in the world, but if we're living a life where one or more of our personal or professional relationships is in a shambles because of miscommunication, lack of communication, or any type of unhealthy communication, we are carrying a very heavy burden indeed.

The Iroquois Nation, the oldest living democracy on earth, got it right. Hundreds of years ago they declared that the best way to move forward with important issues was to consider the effects their decisions would have on seven generations in the future.

What will it mean to our businesses, society, and our families seven generations from now if we continue our tendency away from healthy inter-personal communication? Heck, what will it all look like a mere two generations from now if we don't stop this trend soon? Whenever we choose immediate gratification (peace/comfort) over the opportunity to expand and grow, we may be sated in the short term, but what happens later?

Professionally, if we don't focus on communicat-ing effectively, we might be pleased with the results of our bottom line in the short term, but we miss the opportunity to create healthier work-forces where employees are able to innovate, con-tribute, and feel like they belong and matter.

Personally, if we choose to 'suck it up', remain pas-sive, be overly aggressive, or do whatever we need to avoid uncomfortable conversations, our most-precious relationships can weaken and even become riddled with resentment or estrangement.

Whether we wish to elevate ourselves professionally or we want to sustain healthy, thriving families (or BOTH!), communicating effectively is key. It begins with communicating truthfully, first, with ourselves. Once we establish this critical inner connection, we can move on to communicating truthfully and effectively with others.

I am confident that this is the remedy to the current situation we are in—a society where unhealthy habits are proliferating; where life-enhancing human connections and the element of trust, in business and life, is often elusive.

We must start speaking truthfully; clearing the air and advocating for ourselves and others; and stop choosing the comfort of communicating too passively or aggressively because it is the easier choice.

To build *richer* lives, complete with robust relationships and the ability to ask for what we want and need, we must create healthier communication habits today. We just need the roadmap, the guidebook.

No worries, though! While communicating effectively takes will, skill, and practice, it may take fewer words than you think.

1

Know Your Worth

There is a huge list of reasons why you might be an ineffective and/or passive communicator. Typically, you may choose not to speak because you...

- Don't want to ignite any difficult feelings (in yourself or others)

- Are afraid of how you will be perceived

- Think you will be humiliated if you don't have all the right answers

- Say it is not *worth* the energy or effort

As you move forth in your life and career, look at the word *worth* a little differently and ask yourself...

> – *Are strong relationships worth it?*

> – *Are healthy work environments*

> *worth it?*

> – *Is growing as an individual, **professionally** and **personally**, worth it?*

> – *Are you worth it?*

You can find your voice and speak your truth much more easily if you wholeheartedly know your *worth* first. When you understand your value, clarify what you need, and are able to communicate effectively, you will be much better equipped to reach your goals. You will be closer to being at the cause of your life instead of at the effect.

Your Desired Results

Definition of a *rich* life: A life that includes a healthy amount of money, many healthy relationships, and the healthy ability to communicate.

Sometimes you need to communicate on behalf of yourself so you're able to collaborate effectively, strike a deal, or acquire that elevated position around the board table. Sometimes you need to advocate for others, such as your children, elders, or in your community.

Up until now, speaking and communicating have simply been called 'soft skills.' But ask anyone, and they will affirm that mastering and maintaining effective communication skills is often the most challenging work they'll ever do! Nearly 80% of the population admits to being plagued with some kind of fear of speaking.

The aversion to speaking often permeates one-on-one conversations, too. It is clear that the masses also struggle to speak interpersonally. According to the Social Anxiety Institute, the lifetime prevalence rate of developing this social phobia stands at 13-14%. The good news is the association says you can diminish social anxiety by acquiring new skills and practicing them over time.

Ask yourself, do you sometimes choose to remain either a passive or an aggressive communicator when your *much wiser self* suggests that communicating more effectively might be the key to a major breakthrough?

We get into ruts; communicating ineffectively can become a bad habit.

Take a look at the habits our society is forming around everything from connecting with electronic devices to taking drugs. Speaking effectively and having healthy human interactions are not on the rise—bad habits are. Building a *richer* life by way of speaking truthfully and effectively will continue to diminish.

If you let it.

Let's Begin

I recommend that you write in a journal, a notebook, or on the pages inside this guidebook. Writing will reinforce your learning and allow you to go back to your notes at a later date to track your progress.

Communicate with Yourself

Starting the journey towards becoming a more

effective communicator begins with introspection. Let's find out if you truly **Know Your Worth**.

Ask yourself...

Question: *Do I currently have the **rich** life I want, complete with a healthy amount of money, healthy relationships, and the healthy ability to speak and communicate?*

Answer:

Take your time here. Answering this and the following important questions will help you gauge your starting point before you determine where you'd like to go and grow.

Examples:

> **Personally:** You might want to become more influential so you can broach challenging subjects with someone at home.

Professionally: You might want to try to master a formal presentation or engage in a challenging conversation to enhance your status or build a more cohesive workplace.

Your Communications Foundation

Having a good communication foundation has nothing to do with how you were raised. Plenty of people who were raised in families that didn't focus on verbal communication have mastered what it takes to become more influential and effective. Effective communication is *learned* and gets easier with the right skills and practice.

A strong communication foundation begins with understanding and abiding by two rules: **The Golden Rule** and **The Silver Rule.**

You know **The Golden Rule**: *Do Unto Others As You Would Have Them Do Unto You.* As you speak and communicate, do you try to open the lines of communication instead of shutting people down? Do you work to ensure that no one is purposefully hurt in the process? Do you consistently seek win/win/wins for all parties involved as you communicate? This is **The Golden Rule.**

Seeking win/win/wins is a powerful process, helps you envision the larger picture (like what will happen in the future), and proves that there are always at least three sides to every communication story.

Examples:

> **Personally,** you are looking for wins for:
>
> 1. You.
>
> 2. The person(s) with whom you're speaking.
>
> 3. Family members, your domestic partner, or whoever else is being affected.
>
> **Professionally,** you are looking for wins for:
>
> 1. You.
>
> 2. The person(s) with whom you're speaking.
>
> 3. The company; your department, and/or your clients or whoever else is listening.

The second rule of effective communication is called **The Silver Rule. The Silver Rule** is a simplified version of *The Serenity Prayer*:

"Let us accept the things we cannot change, have the courage to change the things we can, and the wisdom to know the difference."

~Reinhold Niebuhr, author

Silver Energy

The Silver Rule will help you quickly determine what to focus your *energy* on. Energy drains quickly when you attempt to focus on issues you have little or no control over, like:

- Trying to change people

- Pushing too hard in an effort to spur action

As an effective communicator, you know not to waste time and energy trying to force change or regulate anyone but yourself. You will need to navigate uncomfortable conversations, articulate your boundaries, and ask for what you want and need. AND you must do this knowing the only person you have any control over:

You.

Trust in Communication

As an effective communicator, you also know that you will gain the greatest amount of influence by becoming someone others want to be around; someone people trust.

Trust begins when you seek win/win/wins. It continues to build when you consistently work to communicate effectively.

People will respond to your communication efforts, even when there is discomfort, if they perceive that your motives are not totally self-serving (i.e., you are following **The Golden Rule**), that you respect who they are as worthy individuals (**The Silver Rule**), and are courageous enough to speak your truth. People who are able to speak their truth trust themselves. Trusted, effective communicators have a greater ability to become people of influence.

Professionally: More than 60% of employees say they do not **trust**

that their managers honestly care about them

Personally: 50% of all marriages fail because of a lack of **trust.**

Vulnerable = Real and Relatable

Effective communicators are also brave enough to occasionally share their vulnerabilities. How do you do that?

Examples:

> 1. By being well aware of the communication tendencies that come easily to you and the ones that do not.
>
> 2. By sharing stories of times when you faltered.
>
> 3. By asking more questions, listening well, and becoming well aware of the importance of being a lifelong learner.

You can become a more effective communicator when you're occasionally vulnerable because your listeners will easily relate. This helps them begin to relax. This is when trust between you and your listeners starts to emerge.

When you begin to communicate vulnerably, you may experience some discomfort, but you understand this is how you are able to build true connections. Being truthful and occasionally vulnerable enables additional *energy* between you and your listeners to permeate.

Question: *Is it easy for you to share your vulnerabilities with others, **personally** and **professionally**?*

Answers:

Today:

3 months:

What has changed?

6 months:

What has changed?

One year:

What has changed?

Trust and Security

It is imperative that we provide feedback to people as we navigate important projects and issues, **personally** and **professionally**. When done right, truthful feedback can actually instill security into a relationship. But if feedback is conducted improperly, it can shut down the lines of communication. If we avoid providing feedback, however, we never give the lines of communication the opportunity to open.

Choosing NOT to provide feedback can be a great disservice to:

- The people who need it (they often don't

know there's a problem unless you tell them)

• The department or company (**professionally**)

• The family or your relationship (**personally**)

• You (this is your opportunity to be an effective leader, **professionally** and **personally**, and become closer to the cause of your life!)

Here are some guidelines for providing feedback that will support you in seeking win/win/wins. Use some or all of these based on who you are speaking with and what type of infraction needs correcting.

1. Envision your best-case outcome (as you seek a win/win/win)

Example: At the end of the conversation, the person you are speaking with will learn and grow, your department (**professionally**) or family (**personally**) will have overcome an obstacle, and you will have taken steps towards becoming a more effective communicator.

2. Start with a positive comment; commend the person for some recent action or mention a project that's going well.

3. Establish agreement that there is indeed a problem. Define it. Articulate who it is effecting and what it is hindering.

4. Remind the person that making mistakes and having to overcome challenges is a NORMAL part of living/working.

5. Ask what they see as a remedy to the problem. LISTEN.

6. Describe the steps that need to be taken to fix the problem.

7. Ask them to reiterate the steps that should be taken. (This ensures understanding has taken place and gives them another opportunity to speak).

8. Share a personal story of how you overcame a similar issue (mistakes are necessary in life!). This helps you end this

uncomfortable conversation on a positive note. *This is an opportunity for you to be truthful and even a bit vulnerable, which opens the lines of communication and allows trust to flow through.*

When you provide feedback or engage in any uncomfortable conversation, remember, you are seeking win/win/wins, NOT perfection. There's no such thing in communication! Of course, you do not want to sound scripted, but, like a formal presentation, it's always best to prepare by having a plan of action and practicing.

Think, plan, and write first. Ad-lib later.

When communicating with someone who attempts to change the subject that you have brought up, it is your job to be mindful of this and keep the conversation on track. Continue to ask questions and bring them back to the subject at hand. This takes time and energy, especially if you're communicating with people who try to avoid taking responsibility.

From time to time, providing feedback is as simple as saying, "don't do that, do this." It can be that easy *if* trust is already in place. If you are in the process of building or strengthening a trusted relationship, you will want to take more time and utilize additional guidelines.

Choosing to provide feedback will help you avoid having to deal with the issue again. Remember, quite often the last thing people want to do is communicate! So, ask more questions in an effort to get them to talk. Navigating the process of providing feedback will also help you practice the challenging (but vital) skills of listening and being open to learning.

~Constructive Feedback~

It is imperative to provide proactive or constructive feedback if you are to truly know your worth.

You Are Worth It

Being mindful of your strengths, natural tendencies, and areas that need improvement is another crucial element in **Knowing Your Worth**.

Exercise:

Take a Communications Inventory

Create two lists—One that depicts your communication strengths and the other depicting your communication challenges—or where you might be vulnerable and need additional skills.

Example:

> **STRENGTHS**: "I am intelligent and courageous. I have good eye contact with the people with whom I communicate. I dress nicely." (How you dress is important, nonverbal communication).

> **VULNERABILITIES**: "I over-commit. I get tongue-tied when my boss (or sister or colleague...) is around." Or, "I keep speaking when I know I should stop and be silent."

Continue to write and create lists that are as thorough as possible. You may want to ask a trusted friend or colleague to assess your skills and help you refine your lists.

My communication strengths are:

1.

2.

3.

4.

5.

6.

My communication vulnerabilities are:

1.

2.

3.

4.

5.

6.

Now, sit back and "know and own who you are."
You may as well take a few deep breaths while you're at it.

Remember, every human comes complete with strengths and vulnerabilities.

Reminder: YOU *are the most important person with whom to communicate as you seek to wholeheartedly*

Know Your Worth.

More Writing—Keep It Simple

Writing about your strengths and vulnerabilities can uncover extensive areas of your life to improve upon. Pause for a moment. Now, take your list and choose one or two vulnerabilities. Perhaps you know you would benefit greatly by:

(**Personally**) Learning the most effective way to ask for something important to you.

(**Professionally**) Opening the lines of communication with an employee or colleague.

These two challenges are more than enough to tackle simultaneously. Plus, if you keep things simple as you begin, you will be much better able to track your progress. Learn one new skill or technique at a time, THEN move onto greater challenges as you continue to **Know Your Worth** and build your *richer* life.

Question: *What is your first communication goal (**professional** or **personal**)?*

Answer:

Question: *What is your second communication goal (**professional** or **personal**)?*

Answer:

Be Who You Are—2.0

No matter what your current strengths and vulnerabilities, YOU are fine! EVERYONE has both. Do

NOT call your vulnerabilities weaknesses. Having vulnerabilities does not mean you are weak. Your vulnerabilities are conditions you were born with or have learned through conditioning.

Now, REST.

Do not rush through this process. Consider that speaking and communicating comes more naturally to some than others; take time to gauge how easy or challenging communication is for you. Remember, it takes time and effort to do this important work. Slow down so you can acquire, maintain, and emanate as much good energy as possible!

We communicate in many ways:

words, body language, listening, and ***energy.***

Question: *Can you make light of your vulnerabilities—or talk about them with others? Reminder, everyone has them.*

Answer:

YOUR Rich Life

What kind of life do you really want?

If you catch yourself trying to imitate the *rich* life of someone else (a sibling, friend, or colleague), be mindful of this. Many of us are so busy trying to keep up with those around us, we're not even aware of what constitutes our own *rich* life. So, take more time here. YOU are worth it! There is an investment of effort, time, and energy as you dig deeply into **Knowing Your Worth**.

Your personal hopes and desires are uniquely and authentically yours. So, think, uncover, and discover them.

Examples of Your Own Rich Life: Running road races! Landing that CEO position! Serving the homeless! Having GREAT friends at work! Having a family that laughs a lot! Cruising the Caribbean! Harvesting vegetables! Five-caret diamond jewelry (we do not judge—clarify what YOUR rich life looks like and how you gauge YOUR worth. You CAN wear diamonds, feed the homeless, and become the CEO!)

Imagine never taking the time to find out what your unique passions are and what elements you'd like to include in YOUR best, *richest* life. You'll be much more apt to reach your goals and build a life that you love if you know what you want – and don't want – first.

Question: *What kind of elements would you like to include in your* **richer** *life? (**Remember, a rich life = money, relationships, the ability to speak and communicate**). Take your time here.*

Answers (Professionally and Personally):

1.

2.

3.

4.

5.

6.

7.

8.

9.

10.

Question: *What kind of elements do you NOT want in your **richer** life? What are your deal breakers? Take your time here.*

Answers (Professionally and Personally):

1.

2.

3.

4.

5.

6.

7.

8.

9.

10.

As time goes on, what constitutes your *richer* life will evolve.

Question: *How much time and attention are you going to devote to being mindful of communicating effectively* (with yourself and others)? *How are you going to do this?* (I recommend you prioritize this time and create a special space for rest and reflection).

Answers:

Feel, Deal, Heal

We are becoming a society that lives in a state of distraction and "being busy all the time." This human condition appears to be escalating. If indeed you want to break through to your *richer* life, you must first invest time into slowing down enough to be aware of how you are feeling.

Once you sit still for a while (several minutes, a few times per day, electronic-free, if possible), honor and notice how you FEEL about what is and is not working well. You will be much better able to begin to DEAL (sharpen and practice your new communication skills) and finally HEAL what is holding you back from **Knowing Your Worth, Finding Your Voice,** and **Speaking Your Truth.**

Warning: *Your first attempt to **feel** might lead you to habits that enable you to avoid feeling!*

Human Habits:

Ingestible Habits: Alcohol, tobacco, drugs, food (from carbs to coffee to sugar, etc.).

Process Habits: Work, gambling, co-dependency, sex, shopping, perfectionism, sports, Internet (*electronic addictions are increasing rapidly*).

Mature Communication

Here's what might happen when you begin to communicate with yourself, assess your strengths and vulnerabilities, feel, and attempt to become a more effective communicator: You might begin to blame others for your inability to communicate.

Are there challenging people with whom you must occasionally interact?

Yes.

Might you sometimes be intimidated or frustrated by them?

Yes.

Can you choose not to speak or confront these people at this time?

Yes.

Your Choice

Sometimes your decision NOT to communicate is the right one. But choosing not to communicate might keep you from your *richer* life. Remember, the best way to increase your self-worth is to take total responsibility for your communication skills and self-esteem. Feel some fear (it's not easy being human/communicating) and move towards it anyway.

Question: *Do you believe you could become a more effective communicator if someone else would change? If so, explain.*

Answer:

Question: *Do you have any control over what you just described? (**The Silver Rule**). If so, what could YOU do differently?*

Answer:

Here's the Key

Being able to address intimidating or challenging people will absolutely enhance your life and career. Communicating courageously and consistently will propel you towards **Knowing Your Worth** and your *richer* life.

Pedestal Syndrome: When you place someone on a pedestal you remain below them.

Body, Mind, Spirit

(Optional and Recommended)

This communications guidebook does not focus on physical fitness. But, as you dig deeper to truly **Know Your Worth**, please choose to eat right, exercise often, drink lots of water, get enough sleep, breathe deeply and often, clear your mind daily (through a mindful practice, walking in nature, or doing something you love), and greatly

limit (or eliminate, if you're prone to habits) smok-
ing, the intake of sugar or alcohol, any excessive
connection with electronics, or anything else that
is habit-forming.

A healthy body and clearer mind will surely
enhance your journey towards your *richer* life.

Self-care starts you on your path to self-worth.
Self-care will give you energy...the energy needed
to communicate effectively!

Self-care needs to be consistent for the best result.

Call in the Troops

(Optional and Recommended)

Effective communicators know that the work of
Knowing Your Worth takes time, energy, and dili-
gence. It can also be tiring and much easier to
revert to antiquated habits. So why not call in the
troops? God, Buddha, Allah, Angels, Masters, or
whomever or whatever.

Everyone has access to a higher self, an inner elder,

or maybe even a Higher Power. Recommendation: Tap into Him or Her or It...as often as you can for support, strength, comfort, and divine direction.

"Our Father, Mother, Oh Holy One, Angels, OM, etc., I AM SO grateful I do not have to navigate this challenging work alone. Amen."

Last Words on Finding Your Worth

Everyone on earth struggles with some form of insecurity. Doctors, CEOs, and astronauts are ALL occasionally insecure. You are in good company!

Like the gravitational pull towards habits, it's your job, and nobody else's, to notice and curb any pull towards feeling unworthy.

EVERYONE, on occasion, feels awkward when they communicate.

~~~~~~~~~~~~~~~~

Question:

On a scale of 1-10, how do you rate your self-worth?

Answers:

Today:

3 months:

What has changed?

6 months:

What has changed?

One year:

What has changed?

The most effective way to maintain self-worth, is to consistently take actions that scare you (like practicing challenging conversations and/or presentations).

Find Your Voice—The Bridge

Now that you are on your way to your *richer* life and well aware of your communication strengths and vulnerabilities, begin to speak about them out loud. Try practicing this alone (yes, talk to yourself) and then with friends. For the first 90 seconds or so, talk about some of the things you're good or great at (your strengths). For the next 90 seconds or so, talk about some areas in which you struggle (your vulnerabilities).

Question: *Is it easier to talk about your strengths or your vulnerabilities?*

Answer:

After training thousands over the decades, it's clear that the majority of people have a much easier time talking about areas in their lives they wish were different—where they are vulnerable. In order to live a *richer* life through **Knowing Your Worth** and **Finding Your Voice**, be well aware of this! Then think about something that you are great at—something that makes you credible—and begin to talk about it.

Speaking about yourself in high regard often feels awkward or conceited, but it is imperative that you are able to articulate your accomplishments so others are well aware of them. Write and then speak about your strengths—every day if you can—so you become more comfortable with this skill. It is certain to propel your life and career forward.

The time to know your worth and promote yourself is NOW. Waiting for someone else to notice you or help you build your *richer* life means it may never materialize.

Camaraderie

When you begin to communicate with others about effective communication, you will quickly find you have many friends and colleagues who are also challenged by speaking their truth, in both personal and professional settings.

Knowing that so many others struggle with communicating effectively can lead to more dedication to do this work. Might you have friends and colleagues now who are also determined to make effective communication the catalyst for their much *richer* lives?

The best way to **Find Your Voice** is to know that it is already there! So, **Know Your Worth** (this is a discipline). And keep practicing.

Effective communicators do not fake it 'til they make it. They make it so they don't have to fake it.

Case Study:

Casey is an intelligent and well-educated professional who navigated a great position as a regional program manager at a well-respected health care organization. She developed a pilot program intended to support patients and their families, and her colleagues.

She was offered the opportunity to formally present her program and its findings. As she prepared, she learned there would be 10 people in the room, including the company's marketing executive and lawyer.

Casey created a dynamic PowerPoint, checked all her data, and even incorporated music into her presentation. In preparation of her big day, she rehearsed what she was going to say with a few colleagues and her boss, who helped her make a few tweaks. Overall, she was ready, but something kept getting in the way.

Casey kept second-guessing herself. It was a debilitating habit that stressed her out and wasted her time and energy.

Casey had a relentless *criticizer* in her head that kept saying, "Oh, Casey, what are you doing now?" We determined the origins of this *criticizer*. It was a voice from the past—one she often heard while growing up. It was a voice that came from Casey's mother who, unfortunately, didn't encourage Casey to be her authentic self. Instead, her mother had been exasperated at the fact that Casey was a quite unique and very spirited child! Casey's mother was not a bad person. She, like many other parents, wished Casey would be more like she was. But Casey's personality was different—a little more like her dad's side of the family.

What did Casey have control over? The nagging voice in her head was a bit chronic, but with awareness and acceptance, Casey knew she could quiet it. It was something she could control.

After identifying that Casey had a *criticizer*, we agreed that we were not going to allow the *criticizer* to control Casey's opportunity to shine at work.

Even though Casey was experiencing chronic negative self-talk, she knew she had some great strengths. She described herself as a go-getter and relentless in her pursuit of what she wanted.

The next step Casey needed to take was to engage her internal *coaches.* These were more positive voices inside her head that supported and encouraged her and gave her energy.

We began to control her *criticizer* by giving Casey's inner nagging voice a name.

Because of a silly book Casey read when she was a child, she decided to call her *criticizer* Jenny. In this children's book, Jenny was a woman whose head was attached by a simple scarf. If her scarf were to be removed, Jenny's head would fall off!

While Jenny was silly for Casey to ponder and discuss, identifying her as the *criticizer* made her real and easier to wrangle. Being consciously aware of Jenny made Casey realize that Jenny was getting in the way of her *richer* life, and Jenny needed to be eradicated!

Like any nagging voice that slows you down and tries to keep you from your *richer* life, it will return time and time again. So, it's your job to be mindful of it and then quiet it, consistently. When it returns (and it will) it is your job to repeat this process—choose differently—so **Your Worth,** who you *really are* emerges victorious. Breaking this habit is something you have control over (**The Silver Rule**).

Change the habit of negative thinking. Create new neuropathways in your brain through awareness and a mindful practice.

–Tara Bennett-Goleman

Once the *criticizer* was quieter, Casey's own voice

and her *coaches' voices* could be heard. Now, Casey and I could get to work on the details of her presentation.

Casey's formal presentation was way too full. We determined what could be edited so her listeners could easily understand and digest the information she was sharing. Once Casey's nagging voice, Jenny, was quieted, we focused on matching Casey's words and phrasing with her listeners so she could best relate with them. This helped Casey become more influential because her listeners would sense she took time to understand their needs, concerns, and goals.

Casey was quite passionate about her subject matter. With Jenny quiet (not gone, just sitting in the corner), Casey focused on presenting her work. She began to practice articulating how her pilot program would be a great benefit for all *(win/win/win)*. Casey knew Jenny would appear when she delivered her presentation, but when she did, Casey could simply slow down a bit, push the negative thoughts aside, and continue.

Acknowledging Jenny eventually made Casey laugh and helped her feel much more in control of creating and delivering a successful presentation.

Casey focused on the theme of her presentation, the structure of her words and phrases, plus pauses she chose to add. She practiced and worked hard to deliver her presentation naturally. She was also able to become more *present* with her audience instead of focusing on her *criticizer* who typically is overly concerned with perfection and perception and blocks the personal connection between speaker and listener.

Casey's presentation lasted nearly 90 minutes. It was not the best one she would ever do. But it was the start of Casey truly **Knowing Her Worth, Finding Her Voice,** and **Speaking Her Truth.**

Was Casey anxious before she delivered her formal presentation? Of course she was! But she anticipated that fear and worked to turn it into an opportunity to communicate effectively. She had a great passion for her work and she knew that the passion, combined with her effort and newfound ability to communicate, was the gateway to building a much *richer* life.

Casey was faced with this great opportunity to showcase her work and she was not going to let it slip by. Speaking before this group was a big deal. Casey combined two years of her work and presented it to some well-respected and powerful decision makers.

After Casey's presentation, here's what she wrote:

"My audience definitely 'felt' what I was sharing with them. I am flying home now with a smile on my face and feeling blessed for having taken the time to dare greatly."

Casey's program is in the process of being rolled out. Whether it permeates through the entire company or not, she is certain the steps she took towards **Knowing Her Worth, Finding Her Voice,** and **Speaking Her Truth** were life-enhancing AND career-enhancing experiences.

Her new tools will also support her the next time she faces a formal presentation or uncomfortable conversation—like asking for what she wants and has earned!

Question: *Has Casey's story provided you any ideas for Knowing Your Worth, Finding Your Voice, andSpeaking Your Truth? If so, what are they?*

Answers:

2

The Six Pillars Of Effective Communication

THE FOUNDATION

So, you're ready to talk. Perhaps it's a formal presentation at work—or maybe it's a very important, but challenging, discussion with a boss, a family member, or someone you encounter often. How do you prepare, get focused, and deliver your message as clearly, effectively, and relaxed as possible?

The Six Pillars of Effective Communication is a support system. It gives you the tools to help you connect with and communicate with your audience in any type of environment, while delivering your message in a way that is true to your style and feels comfortable with who you are. *The Six Pillars of Effective Communication* will support and guide you—whether you're speaking one-on-one or before a large group.

Before digging in, ask yourself: When my presentation or conversation is complete, what will I have accomplished? Think of your best-case scenario.

Questions:

1. How will the other person, the group, or your audience feel?

2. What else or who else will be affected?

3. What will your audience learn, understand, agree to, or be ready to take action on?

Answers:

1.

2.

3.

Questions: How will you feel after successfully delivering a formal presentation (**professional**) or engaging in a challenging conversation (**professional** or **personal**)? Will you feel relieved, proud, better about the situation, or simply glad that you courageously spoke your truth?

Answers:

1.

2.

3.

As with creating anything that has yet to materialize, you cannot reach a positive outcome until you
envision a positive outcome.

"Imagination is more valuable than knowledge."
—*Albert Einstein*

If you take time to envision what the positive outcome looks and feels like, your odds of success
increase dramatically. So, take a moment to both
see and anticipate how communicating more
effectively will change your life and career for the
better.

Pillar #1: Know and Own and BE Who You Are

Effective communication begins with the study of
people—first and foremost, yourself. Think about
your natural tendencies. Are you left-brained and
more reserved or right-brained and more outgoing?

Are you a linear communicator who focuses on facts, figures, and details to make your point, or are you a creative communicator who uses images, feelings, and metaphors or analogies?

In whichever category you fall, *The Six Pillars of Effective Communication* will help you maximize your power to communicate, regardless of your starting point. Whichever traits you begin with are fine. For the most part, your personality traits are something you were born with and you can't alter them much. These traits are quite important—they help you be uniquely you—complete with your own strengths and vulnerabilities.

Your job is to be mindful of your personality traits and to know what you can and cannot change.

What you can change is how comfortable you feel about yourself.

The first step towards feeling comfortable with yourself is to accept yourself as you are, then commit becoming the most effective communicator you can become. In other words, where you think you are weak, don't criticize yourself towards improvement. Instead, learn new skills and then COACH yourself towards improvement. Encourage yourself as you would your best friend or a person you are mentoring.

Doing this is some of the most-important communications work you'll ever do.

When you focus more on your attributes than your perceived weaknesses you will naturally find yourself playing to your strengths and this will help you become more confident. Knowing and owning the worthy person you are is the first step towards maximizing your ability to communicate. This pillar enables you to be authentically YOU so you can take the steps necessary to create your *richer* life through effective communication.

Pillar #2: Relate with Your Listeners

One of the greatest and most effective communicators in history was Abraham Lincoln. He seemed to understand the importance of Pillar #2 when he said, "When I get ready to talk, I spend 2/3 of the time thinking about what they need to hear and 1/3 thinking about what I want to say."

This means once he knew what he wanted to communicate, he thought about who his listeners were—what they needed to hear, and the language he needed to use so they could relate to him as a trusted leader.

All of this was done within the parameters of his natural style. President Lincoln often struggled with what he perceived to be his vulnerabilities, but he knew his strengths and, more importantly, wrote and delivered his talks with the intent of getting into the heads and hearts of his audience so he could influence and inspire them to action.

As you continue to study people and how they are inspired by communicators who are authentic, you'll find there are numerous personality types. According to Drs. Tony Alessandra and Michael O'Connor, authors of the book *The Platinum Rule*, there are four basic types of people and what motivates each is different:

> **Director**—Motivated by those who are efficient and competent
>
> **Socializer**—Motivated by those who are interested in them
>
> **Relater**—Motivated by those who are warm and sincere
>
> **Thinker**—Motivated by those who are thorough and well prepared

You'll benefit greatly from tweaking your communication and your language based on how your listeners are influenced.

All people relate more easily to people who have

similar personality traits. While it is always important to be your authentic self, it's imperative that what you say resonates with the other person or the people in the group! So, do your best to get a sense of who they are and what inspires them.

Also, your listeners have a specific energy, and so do you! Be cognizant of the energy in the room. Work to keep it positive and more focused on them and less on yourself.

Example: If you're a right-brained extrovert and you're speaking to a crowd of, say, accountants or IT professionals who can often be left-brained and more reserved, you may want to quiet the energy that you emanate a bit.

Meanwhile, if you are more reserved and you are speaking with listeners who are more outgoing, do not think you must carry on a high-energy, articulate conversation at all times. In this case, you will actually become more influential and able to increase your effectiveness by asking more questions and focusing on their emotions.

Asking more questions, even in the case of a formal presentation, will help maintain the connection between you and your listeners.

Studies show less than 10% of the words we speak are retained. Therefore, an integral part of effective communication is being aware of the style and energy of your listeners. So, in preparation of your next opportunity to communicate something important, ask yourself, "who are they?" and "what do they need?" You always want to speak in a way that relates to your listeners as naturally as possible. When you do, your listeners will innately know you've taken time to understand and relate with them.

This is how you begin to serve your listeners. Pillar #2 provides great support in helping you attain your desired result.

Know Your Worth AND THEIR Worth

Pillar #3: Master Your Content

Whether you're ready to communicate a story, an elevator pitch, or a keynote speech; or you're preparing for a vital discussion; invest time into jotting down what you want to say. This will help you win the attention of your listeners because you'll be sharing information that's well organized and relevant.

You may find that writing things down leads to throwing away the first draft and then writing it down again. As you do so, remember to remain authentically YOU while choosing words that are easily relatable with your listeners. The most memorable conversations and presentations are the ones that areauthentic and easy to understand.

When you are authentic or real with your listeners, your listeners will *really* listen to you. They will both feel and hear what you are saying and your authenticity helps them trust and connect with you. When you create an environment of connectedness, you create an environment that maximizes your ability to communicate.

We've all listened to people who think they're communicating and connecting, but in reality, they're just talking. Unless both speaking AND understanding is taking place, true communication will remain limited.

In preparing your content, avoid excessive industry jargon or extraneous details—because most people are unable to retain a huge amount of new information. We're all living in a society of communication overload, so have mercy!

People remember what they are able to digest and understand. They remember how we inspire them, what we encourage them to think about, and how we make them feel. So, take a chance and give them something they don't expect—like a laugh,or hope, or your new perspective on an interesting topic. Give them YOUR TRUTHFULNESS while you give them your IDEAS, especially if you're working to influence change.

Then rehearse. And rehearse again.

> **Professionally:** Especially if it is a formal presentation.

> **Personally:** YES, it's more than fine to write and prepare, especially if you are poised to have a strategic and challenging conversation.

Some people rehearse in the mirror—others talk to themselves as they're driving or walking. Do whatever works for you. But do it nonetheless. Work out all the tongue twisters, make sure you get people's names correct, practice being relaxed, and envision the positive outcome that you're determined to have. This way, when the time comes to communicate, your energy is right, you are speaking naturally, you do not sound stiff or stressed, you're confident of the subject matter, you are able to pace yourself, and your words flow.

Pillar #4: Anticipate Questions and Reactions

You're getting closer now to delivering your presentation or having your challenging discussion, but before you do, ask yourself a few questions, starting with, "What am I missing?"

Put yourself into the shoes of your listeners and ask yourself, "Am I being authentic; memorable? As they receive my words, how will they feel? Will they wonder about anything along the way?"

Truly effective speakers and communicators do their best to be as thorough as possible; to be able to answer any and every question that will ever be posed. However, the time will come, guaranteed, when something comes up that you are unable to answer. What do you do then?

Let honesty prevail. Remember, you are confident and comfortable with your command of the subject because you've taken the time to be thoughtful and prepared. If a question comes up that you either haven't anticipated or don't know the answer to, remain composed and professional while politely telling your listeners, "I don't know, BUT I'm going to get that answer!"

Or ask them what THEY believe is the answer. You can also give them the part of the answer you are confident about and then promise to engage them at a later date. People know we are undergoing an unprecedented time of change and sometimes data or facts evolve quickly. Be truthful (aka **Speak Your Truth**).

In the case of a challenging discussion, whether it be providing feedback or asking for a sale, your audience will acquire the sense that you're seeking a win/win/win, (which you are), if you wrap up the conversation with a question such as, "Are we missing anything?"

After you pose this question, become present, focused, and attentive. Become comfortable in the silence.

This question will prove that, while you have high integrity, you are not infallible. It will communicate that you are a truthful person and that you are confident enough to show that you are always open to learning (your chance to be vulnerable).

Communicators who are courageous enough to be as vulnerably truthful as possible are people who can be trusted. If you can only be partially transparent, say so—be truthful about it. People are greatly influenced by candor.

Anticipating questions and envisioning reactions are powerful tools to use as you prepare to build connections with your listeners.

Using these tools will help you evolve from someone who is simply speaking, to a person who is able to influence and build trusted relationships.

EVERY time you communicate, you have a chance to diminish or strengthen your relationships.

Pillar #5: Serve While Speaking

Nerves often kick in as you begin to speak. Fear and insecurities can be acute and you can feel very uncomfortable and awkward. You may even begin to question everything you have done up to that point.

This is natural. It happens to everyone to one degree or another. But, if you make one small shift here, you'll be much better able to speak powerfully and with much greater ease. Think about educating and serving your audience instead of being overly concerned with how you look or sound.

A communicator who places him or herself into service mode as a teacher, instead of someone who's delivering 'the perfect words,' is much more apt to connect with listeners by exuding a confident, caring command of the subject.

Effective communicators never talk down to their listeners, and they don't put their listeners on a pedestal. They place themselves on a level playing field and strive to be of service and of value to their listeners.

Effective communicators know...

> 1. They are doing their best. They may be subject matter experts, but they're always open to learning.
>
> 2. Their most important jobs are to be understandable, relatable, and approachable.
>
> 3. Everyone is different. Different people learn differently and at different paces and some are more prone to learning than others. So, while the communicator's goal is to educate and inspire 100% of their listeners 100% of the time, they know this is impossible. That's because effective communication is a vital part of creating a *richer* life and career, but it is not an exact science.

Remember, even the greatest communicators will not nail it every time. This is a challenging fact for many, especially those in predominantly left-brain-oriented fields (sorry accountants, tech professionals, and others who skew more analytical), yet very valuable to accept.

As you continue to refine your communication skills, here are a few additional tips.

> 1. Posture matters. With good posture, you will feel more powerful and you'll be able to

breathe better. Plus, you will appear more self-assured and confident.

2. Practice. Rehearse. Repeat. You WILL be prepared!

3. Slow down and insert silence. Silence and pausing allows your listeners to digest the information you're sharing. It also gives them a chance to feel what you're feeling about a specific subject. Slowing your pace also gives you the opportunity to *read and understand* how your listeners are faring while you are speaking.

If you sense the people you are speaking with are getting bored or agitated, perhaps it's time to change things up. Have them answer a question. Throw in something humorous, share an anecdote, or simply ask them how they're doing with what you are communicating.

The most-effective communicators maintain eye contact and connection with their listeners. This way, the people you are speaking with are much more apt to remain engaged, feel your energy, and retain the information that's being shared. Effective communicators keep their listeners part of the conversation (a presentation is a conversation with structure) and make sure they're not a separate entity. Remember, we're all in this together—as you seek win/win/wins while speaking.

Pillar #6: Detach from the Outcome

Detaching from the outcome doesn't mean you don't care. It means that you care so much about communicating effectively that you will not concern yourself about delivering whatever you are sharing perfectly. You also will not over-stress about how you and your messages will be received.

You have already worked diligently to be as prepared and thorough as possible by navigating Pillars #1-5!

Instead of remaining attached to the outcome, *trust* that the work you put into preparing was good work. *Trust* your grasp of the subject matter. *Trust* that you have taken time to think about everyone concerned.

Building trust with others begins with trusting yourself.

When you trust yourself, you become more confident and comfortable.

When you are confident and comfortable, your listeners will be much more comfortable, too. *How you feel is directly related with how you make your listeners feel.*

If, while you are speaking, your mind is saying something like, "Oh no, what are they thinking?" or "Did I say the correct words?" please understand that your *criticizer* may be getting in the way. When it does (and it will!), notice it and *thank it* (it's trying to protect you, but can sabotage instead).

Then, push it away. This will help you maintain the powerful connection that you have generated between you and your listeners.

Choose to remain composed; to remain the incredibly WORTHY person you are.

Effective communicators choose to be guided by their higher self; inner elder; internal coach, not their criticizer.

Being attached to the outcome and being concerned with perception or perfection is human and normal. So, be aware of these stressful thoughts and, if they are persistent, ask your inner *coaches* for help!

You can replace your worry over perception and perfection with your new focus:

> 1. You are prepared.
>
> 2. You have the skill to stay present with your listeners.

Detaching from the outcome opens the lines of communication wider and allows an even greater energy to flow between you and the people you're speaking with.

When the lines are open wide, human-to-human connections are formed. You can consistently bring higher wisdom into the room. Your connections have an opportunity to flourish. You become more influential. Trust can flow. More win/win/wins occur.

Recommendation: Practice detaching from the outcome immediately before you start your uncomfortable conversation or formal presentation, as this is typically when your angst about speaking is at its highest.

You are prepared, present and able to detach
from the outcome. *If not this, then something better.*

3

The Art Of Speaking, Presenting, And Persuading

THE SYSTEM

There's a small percentage of the population for which communication comes easily and seems to flow. Everyone else must learn effective communication skills.

As you learn to communicate effectively, you'll benefit greatly by acquiring two things:

> 1. A format or template to follow to support what you'd like to say, and

2. An understanding of your communication style (different from your personality style).

Communication Styles:

Passive, Aggressive, Passive/Aggressive, and Assertively Effective.

You may want to take some time and dive deeply into educating yourself about each of these styles, but, simply stated...

Passive Communicators choose not to express their feelings and opinions or assert themselves. Ignoring important issues and opportunities can leave passive communicators behind and feeling anxious, resentful, regretful, or even depressed because they haven't expressed themselves.

Aggressive Communicators advocate for their needs in a domineering and sometimes verbally belittling manner. They can often speak loudly, interrupt frequently, and can insult and alienate the people around them.

Passive/Aggressive Communicators appear outwardly calm as their frustration builds. They act out of exasperation in subtle, subversive, or unexpected ways that seem out of character. By not addressing issues directly and timely, they can alienate themselves from others, and wreak havoc with reprisals.

If you want to become a more influential and effective communicator, you can't begin by being passive or aggressive.

Most passive communicators remain that way for many reasons ranging from fear and insecurities, to over-thinking, to procrastination.

To get beyond passivity, truthfully ask yourself about the importance of what it is you'd like to communicate. When you remain passive, nothing changes. When you decide to speak even while feeling discomfort, the results you'd like to attain become your *cause*, whether you're seeking a raise, a promotion, sharing an innovative idea, driving a project or team at work, or selling something, including yourself.

Aggressive communicators will benefit greatly by being mindful of how this communication style hinders trusted relationships. Aggressive communicators might consider learning about the mindful practice of deep breathing and awareness of thought. This type of practice can help you slow down so you can choose thoughtful responses rather than forceful reactions or manipulative language.

Assertively Effective Communicators are able to clearly state what they need, calmly but firmly share their opinions and ideas, and confidently advocate for their rights and needs without violating the rights of others. **Assertively Effective Communicators** value and respect themselves and others. They expect occasional discomfort, strive to understand it, and overcome it with will, skill, and practice.

―――――――――

Assertively Effective Communicators become more influential because they know their worth, find their voice, and speak their truth.

Assertively Effective Communicators build internal fortitude and know they are able to build confidence and ability through speaking, while seeking win/win/wins.

―――――――――

Preparing to Address Your Listeners

Here's a template to support you in becoming a more effective speaker. It will help you whether you need to deliver an important presentation or are facing a strategic conversation.

The Art of Speaking, Presenting, and Persuading—Template:

- Start from the end

- State your intention

- Make your case

- Reiterate your position

- Make the ask

- Be silent, at least for a moment

You may be wondering why there's a need to write things down if you're preparing to have a challenging conversation.

Personally: If your *cause* is important, then it's deserving of proper preparation. Writing things down will ensure you don't forget to address something important.

Professionally: You will be able to think through your entire conversation or formal presentation as you utilize *The Six Pillars of Effective Communication.*

Let's dig deeper now into the template to help you craft and deliver communication that is compelling, concise, and effective.

Start from the End

When you start from the end, you're taking time to envision your desired result. So ask yourself, "When I'm finished communicating, what is it that I'd like to have happen?" This is your intention.

Example: Say you're hoping you'll receive a promotion, complete with a new title and more money.

Get clear on it. *It is fine to take a moment to prepare for a possible negative outcome. But once you do that, tuck your worst-case scenario away and know it's there if you need it.* Now, envision your best, most-positive outcome.

Know your goal.

Envision a positive outcome.

Then begin.

State Your Intention

Here, you might say something like: "After we discuss my qualifications and ideas and combine them with the needs of the company, I am confident that the decision to promote me into this position will be an easy one."

Remember, when you state your intention, your listeners will be clear about the direction of the conversation. Stating your intention will also simplify and clarify what it is you're ready to communicate. In this very busy and distracted world, this is what your listeners need: communication that is clear, concise, and focused on them.

Consistently ask yourself what is important to your listeners.

State Your Case

Begin the journey of stating your case by writing down a list. Think of this like creating chapters in a book. In order for your listeners to envision your cause or case as clearly as you do, you have to be able to tell them a story that takes them from point A to point B to point C.

Personally: If you're preparing for a short conversation, you may not have to write down and rehearse every word, but be cognizant of where and how you'd like the conversation to flow.

Professionally: If you're planning for a lengthier conversation or formal presentation, you'll want to treat each element like a mini chapter or like its own mini presentation, complete with an opening, body, and ending.

When sharing complex topics, keep your verbiage simple because your goal is to help your listeners understand and retain your information. A lot of business communication fails to connect with listeners because speakers often use too many extraneous details in an attempt to highlight their wealth of knowledge.

———

People are overloaded.

Expedite their time.

<hr>

Reiterate

With the world running on full speed, reiterating is more important than ever. Reiterating is simply restating the message you just delivered. Reiterating can be as simple as repeating your intention and most-important points. You also may want to communicate the benefits the audience will receive by doing business with you **(professionally)** or maintaining your relationship **(personally)**.

Example: In the case of asking for a promotion, you may say something like, "So that is why I know I am the clear choice for this position and why I know I can serve the company and help the department thrive like never before."

Make the Ask

Effective communicators know how to ask for what they want and need. This is where you might find the most discomfort, so take time to determine how best to ask for what you want as naturally and confidently as possible. Write it down. Keep it concise. Then rehearse the words, so when the time comes for you to make the ask, you will not sound scripted. Your words will flow easily.

Anticipate discomfort.

If you don't ask for what you want or need, it will not materialize.

Remember your cause.

Be Assertively Effective.

Stop Talking

The best thing to do after asking for what you want and need is to pause in silence. You will most likely find discomfort in your silence, but this is also where you'll find your POWER! Standing in your powerful silence communicates as much as your words do and allows both you and your listeners to feel your energy and confidence – very desirable attributes in both business and life.

You may want to follow your silent pause (3-5 seconds) with the question, "What do you think are the next best steps?" Or in the case of a more for-mal presentation, pause for a moment then tell them (yes, articulate to your listeners) what you believe are their next best steps. Then you can ask your listeners for buy-in by saying something like, "Envision what this will mean to you."

So, Now What?

There's a good chance that YOU just became more influential. There's a chance that you sold your SELF, your products, and your services! There's a chance that you OPENED the lines of communica-tion.

There's also a chance you didn't.

When you find success, commend yourself for a job well done. When you find that you did not attain your desired result, *hang in there*. Then ask...

Question: *Did I forget a step or miss something as I pre-pared?*

Answer:

If you forgot a step or missed something important, learn from what transpired and try again. Effective communication is a discipline that takes will, skill, and practice.

Question: Were your listeners *ready for* or *open to* what you communicated or asked for?

Answer:

If your listeners were not ready for or open to what you communicated, you will benefit greatly by detaching from the outcome. Sometimes people need time before they're ready to take action.

Sometimes, they will never be ready! (The Silver Rule)

Should you try again? Success often takes many attempts.

⸻

Here are some quick stories about how maximizing your power to communicate greatly supported two professionals who were really struggling with being effective and influential. They both took the following steps in an effort to enhance their communication skills:

> 1. They took time to understand **The Six Pillars of Effective Communication.**

> 2. They took time to use the template and practice so they were more prepared and better able to become present with their listeners so they could become more influential.

Case Study: John's Story

John was an accomplished senior leader who was well respected and successful. He managed a team of health care professionals and communicated fairly easily while speaking one-on-one and in small groups.

One day, John had an opportunity to address a bigger crowd at an event he was planning to attend. Just the thought of preparing to engage this larger audience made him very anxious.

I reminded John that it didn't matter whether he was speaking to 1 person or 1,001 people, you always address a crowd like you're speaking to just one person. Speaking to a larger crowd in this personalized way helps each person feel as though you are giving them individualized attention.

John then followed the template. First, he stared from the end, taking time to envision his desired outcome. He literally closed his eyes and took time to think.

After doing that, John told me that, in a perfect world, by the time his presentation was complete he would be able to introduce a new concept to this audience, bond with as many of the listeners as possible, and have several participants want to meet him at a later date so they could learn more about him and his work.

Once this was clarified, John was ready to state his intention. He began by saying something like, "Good evening! I'm thrilled to be here to tell you about some exciting concepts I know will be a tremendous benefit to you and your organization by helping you save time and money. I'm confident that in just a few minutes, you'll want to learn more about what I am going to introduce. This concept can be described in three simple steps..."

At the end of the presentation, John reiterated his intention and then communicated the action he wanted them to take. After he did so, he paused, for just a moment, while the audience digested what he had shared.

Because John planned what he wanted to say, plugged it into the template, and rehearsed, he did beautifully. You'll be happy to hear that several audience members came up to John after his presentation and asked to learn more about his innovative ideas and for one-on-one consultations, as he had envisioned.

Case Study: Marissa's Story

Like John, Marissa was quite bright and also humble. She worked diligently in her company for more than a decade as a highly sought-after scientist.

But she was challenged.

Marissa had recently been promoted, but she found herself bogged down in her old projects because of the company's workload. When she shared this problem with her boss, she didn't get the results she wanted. When she tried again to address the issue, she was so uncomfortable and frustrated, she actually cried. She felt stuck. Marissa wanted to remedy this issue as quickly as possible and to eventually become a VP in the organization.

But who would hire a VP who cries?

So, the first thing she did was take a step back. She saw all the things that had materialized up to that point were actually *huge opportunities* for her to evolve as a communicator (and a leader).

Marissa skews introverted, so speaking does not flow as easily as it does for people who are more outgoing. And this is OK! That's how she was born. Being introverted is human and normal (According to Susan Cain, author of *Quiet, The Secret Power of Introverts*, 1/3 to 1/2 of all people are introverted).

It also means that when faced with difficult conversations, it's best for Marissa to plan out what she'd like to say and practice before speaking.

Marissa began by pinpointing her strengths and vulnerabilities. Once Marissa clearly saw her value (she was very intelligent, detail-oriented, brave, and direct, and she knew what she wanted to say), she plugged what she wanted to communicate into the template...

Starting from the end, Marissa could envision what she hoped would happen.

She began the conversation by saying so. This statement included the benefits to her, her boss, and the company (win/win/win).

Then she took time to state her case. She spoke clearly, concisely, and with authority. While she did this, she asked for buy-in along the way by saying courageous and truthful things like, "You see that this is not working," and "Thank you for understanding my frustration."

Because her command of the subject matter was so strong and she had taken time to practice everything from understanding her boss's personality style to maintaining good posture to being comfortable while pausing in silence, Marissa was able to open the lines of communication and remain composed and professional.

Marissa wrapped up her difficult conversation by reiterating and asking for what she wanted. She even went so far as to write down a brief outline of what she talked about during this challenging discussion and handed a copy to her boss.

After the conversation, Marissa did not get a VP position. But, she did get the support she needed to begin to work into her newly defined role. Meanwhile, her boss articulated the fact that

Marissa was extremely thoughtful, prepared, and a very effective communicator—which are skills that everyone needs if they want to be hired; promoted; become part of a dynamic, collaborative team; and thrive in business.

This process also provided Marissa with confidence to continue to stand tall in other areas of her life as she continues to **Know Her Worth, Find Her Voice,** and **Speak Her Truth.**

Two years after Marissa learned how to effectively and consistently communicate with her boss and colleagues, she decided it was time to continue her career at a company where she could advance more quickly. She landed a great job at another company in California. Marissa is now a VP.

"Where you have your greatest angst is where you have your greatest opportunity for growth."

~Marianne Williamson

4

Sounding Like A Girl; Acting Like A Guy

(Yin and Yang with Grace)

Gender lines have blurred dramatically over the past few decades. Men and women are equally striving to live *rich* lives complete with money, strong relationships, and the ability to speak and communicate. To achieve a *rich* life, it is imperative that people of all genders acquire the ability to become economically self-sufficient while working inside and outside the home, and often remotely, as well.

This is a tall order. And such is life. Building a *rich* life takes time, balance, energy, and strength. Becoming the most effective communicator you can be will absolutely support you along the way.

While gender lines have blurred, some gender-specific communication habits remain. You will be well served to understand and try to break them.

Remember, communication habits are challenging to change. If you don't try, they can become *vicious cycles*.

The first step towards turning any *vicious cycle* into a *healthy cycle* is awareness.

NOTE: These antiquated communication habits/traits do not affect all females, but years of experience prove they are still quite prevalent.

Women, be aware of the following...

- Placing a question mark at the end your statements

- Lowering your volume when you speak

- Diminishing your value by using words like "little" or "just" while describing your accomplishments

- Apologizing when there's no need to

- Choosing to remain passive or silent

Question: *Do you have any of these communication habits? If so, which ones?*

Answer:

Remember, the first step towards becoming an effective communicator is an inward one. Whether the tendency to communicate this way is innate or learned, it doesn't matter. The question is, "Are you willing to take new steps towards becoming a more effective communicator so you can become the leader of your life and career?"

Blazing New Trails

If you are a woman, be aware of the old-fashioned

tendency of taking care of others before taking care of yourself. There are always going to be people around you who need you, and who you want to help.

If you choose to live a *richer* life, constantly focusing on others first is not going to take you there. Caring for others can actually be habit forming and easier than doing the hard work of navigating your own life by communicating effectively. So, awareness, focus and practice are necessary.

***

Caring for small children, our work, and older parents is crucial.

So is caring for YOU.

***

If you are a seasoned female who already **Knows Her Worth** and is able to **Find Her Voice** and **Speak Her Truth**, encourage your younger counterparts to do the same. Women can accomplish their goals and even attain pay equity across the land, one voice at a time.

As with any important cause, you can acquire quicker results when you teach what you have learned.

One last note. Have you ever heard a woman bad-mouth another behind her back?

Let this not permeate through **ANY** of your relationships. Make the choice to be a positive example for current and future generations of females and males.

Communicate directly, truthfully, effectively. Seek win/win/wins.

Or choose to remain silent. Only you can determine what to stand for or when to stand in your powerful silence.

―――――――――

"Western women will rescue the world."

The Dalai Lama, 2010

―――――――――

Men...

Thank you for being you. Over the past several decades, women have had books and peers with which to commiserate and collaborate as they've navigated the path towards a more fair, equitable, and *richer* life.

You, on the other hand, have figured out how to

continue to evolve as best as you can. And you've done this mostly alone. What do I say to that?

Not an easy process! Like women, you have received mixed messages like, "Become a great provider" and "Why aren't you burping the baby?"

So, men, please hear this, "Keep going!"

How on earth do you do that? Work hard to build your own, authentic *rich* life. Then, like women, rest when you can…

…so you have the energy it takes to communicate effectively!

The healthiest relationships, both **personal** and **professional**, are the ones where all parties are able to **Know Their Worth, Find Their Voices,** and **Speak Their Truth.** So take time, first, to communicate with yourself as to what type of communicator you are. What unique elements do you want and need in your life? Work and negotiate (yes, speak!) to make them happen.

It does not matter what gender you are, the more will, skill, and practice you put into becoming an effective communicator, the *richer* your life will become.

In any relationship, **personal** and **professional**, give-and-take, collaboration and compromise must happen. Our partners (spouses, bosses) in business and life will not know what we want and need unless we tell them.

The communication role models for men have been extremely limited. I am not going to point you in any direction (Tony Robbins? Wayne Dyer? Sports figures?) If you want to pave the path towards a *richer* life, read, understand, and utilize what is in this communications guidebook; it is not gender specific.

This is especially critical if you would like to improve your current communication skills so you can achieve:

More money, healthy, and strong relationships, and the healthy ability to speak and communicate.

Meanwhile, be aware of some communication habits that men are more prone to (*acquired through decades of observation*):

- Interrupting

- Not listening well

- Speaking aggressively

- Being verbose

Instead...

- Ask clarifying and probing questions

- Become more empathetic to others

- Understand various personality styles and the value they contribute

- Work collaboratively and inclusively

You can have all the money in the world, but if you don't have strong relationships and the healthy ability to communicate, your life doesn't feel very rich after all.

The Secret Ingredient – Listening

Because you must collaborate with many people in your life — spouses, bosses, colleagues, family members — **listening** is a vital skill. It is equally as important as the ability to speak. Communication is a two-way street. We send (when we speak) and receive (when we listen).

So, be aware of how you currently listen. Almost everyone—*men and women*—can improve in this area. Listening is a form of respect. Respect leads to trust. Trust is the most important element in all forms of communication.

To sharpen your listening skills, follow these guidelines for the best results:

- Slow down and eliminate distractions

- Make eye contact, lean in

- Write important things down

- Focus sharply instead of planning, judging or wandering – *Turn wandering into wondering. Get curious.*

- Empathize – *Can you feel as they feel?*

- Clarify – *Reiterate. If you're unsure of what you've heard, ask!*

Listening takes time, energy, and effort but there

is a huge ROI (return on investment) when you do it right and do it often.

If you catch yourself becoming distracted and not being a good listener, admit it to the person you are speaking with, apologize, and try again. Be truthful. Practice.

Great Listeners

Effective listening expands your knowledge. It helps you avoid mistakes. And it proves to the person or group that you respect them; that you are working hard to ensure that understanding and connection are taking place.

If one of your relationships needs repair, the first question to ask yourself is, "Am I truly being present and listening deeply to them? Or am I only concerned about my own agenda?"

Question: *On a scale of 1-10, how do you rate your listening skills?*

Answers:

Today:

3 months:

What has changed?

6 months:

What has changed?

One year:

What has changed?

Beginning to Speak Your Truth

Notice how the people around you respond as you transform into becoming a more effective communicator. Some may appreciate your truthfulness and newfound candor! Others—not so much. At first, some may feel discomfort when you broach challenging issues and may try to change the subject, throwing you off course. Understanding, anticipating, and preparing for this will be very beneficial. Practice bringing the subject back on track while remembering your strengths. The more you flex this muscle, the stronger it will become. And, of course, always be open to learning.

Your listeners may not be seeking win/win/wins (yet), but you are. So, remain authentically you (Pillar #1). And remember, detaching from how others respond to anything you do or say will be your constant companion (Pillar #6) as you navigate your *richer* life through effective communication.

Knowing what you stand for and what you will not stand for is vital – for everyone.

Remember, YOU are the only one you can control (**The Silver Rule**). Easier said than done, but it is worth the investment of time and energy to comprehend and master!

Once you get accustomed to communicating effectively (it's a discipline), it gets easier. Here are a few lines you can use during a disagreement:

> • *"That doesn't work for me."*

> • *"When that occurs, here's what's happening for me..."*

- *"Are you open to hearing how I see this differently?"*

- *"I'm having a hard time accepting that. Here's why."*

- *"Help me to understand how this could have happened or what you mean by what you just said."*

Communicating what does and does not work for you is much more effective than telling someone they are wrong. Pointing fingers or hurting someone by using sharp words may actually feel good in the moment (immediate gratification, a habit), but you will not move closer to achieving win/win/wins and communicating effectively.

Effective communication is the foundation of leadership. If we want richer lives; to be closer to the cause and not the effect, *we must lead the way*, professionally and personally.

5

Vicious Cycles And Healthy Cycles

Communicating consistently and effectively is not easy work. It takes great focus and energy. It takes will, skill, and practice. It requires decisive action and courage. It is also required if you want to build and maintain your *richest* life possible.

AND, effective communication is the most vital element to add to your repertoire if you are seeking a more confident existence.

How do you become more confident? You choose

to tackle your toughest challenges! You choose to take chances! You choose to shy away from any kid of immediate gratification.

You choose to **Speak Your Truth**.

Examples:

> **Personally:** Call a friend—perhaps someone with whom you would like a better relationship.

> **Professionally:** Walk into the boss's office and present your innovative ideas.

You could even choose to speak formerly before a large crowd—perhaps something you've never done before.

Effective communication will provide you the foundation for building a *richer* life AND it is the gateway to a more confident existence. A *richer* life consists of what we have AND how we feel.

Effective communication is directly related with so many important human conditions and needs.

And it contributes to breaking the insidious, vicious cycles of:

- Insecurity

- Habits/addictions

- Unhealthy and estranged relationships

- Economic discrepancies

Question: *What are your thoughts about breaking the vicious cycles you are experiencing through communicating more effectively? Take your time here.*

Answer:

6

Choose Well

So, my dear reader, communicate truthfully first with yourself. Then share what you learn with those around you. Teach your children well, too! As the leader of your life (**professionally** and **personally**), your words and actions rub off on others. AND, most importantly, your choices.

> • If you choose to stand up and communicate effectively on behalf of yourself and others, people around you will learn how it's done. Remember, courage is contagious.

• If you choose to remain plugged into electronics or anything else that is habit-forming, that is what you will be modeling for others, including the next generation.

• If you choose to become versed in technology, business, AND effective communication, your mentees (and offspring) will be inspired to follow your example.

• If you choose not to suppress what you are feeling (Feel, Deal, Heal) and work to maximize your power to communicate (instead of giving your power away), you can start to build your *richer* life today.

You have ALL YOU NEED to become a more effective communicator.

Do not expect perfection. Seek excellence.

Practice.

With new skills and over time, the lines of communication will open; your incredible energy will begin to flow.

And so will your *richer* life—AND the lives of future generations.

Know Your Worth

Find Your Voice

Speak Your Truth

Live a *Richer* Life

⸻⸻⸻

Effective communication is a choice.

You CHOOSE to do the work.

⸻⸻⸻

Educated and inspired by many. Special thanks to:

Social Anxiety Institute

Mindfulness Center at Brown University

Tara Bennett Goleman, Emotional Alchemy

Drs. Tony Alessandra and Michael O'Connor, *The Platinum Rule*

Drs. Dennis and Ethan Becker, *The Speech Improvement Company*

Albert Mehrabian, *Silent Messages*

Marianne Williamson. *A Return To Love*

Susan Cain, Quiet, *The Secret POWER of Introverts*

Jeffrey Deckman, *Conscious Leadership Mindset*

Gabrielle Bernstein

Pat Hastings Burns

Brenè Brown

Oprah

Maslow

Jesus

Buddha

"We are what we repeatedly do.

Excellence is not an act, but a habit."

~Aristotle

About The Author

Donna Rustigian Mac is a pioneering female media professional, spending 25+ years in the broadcasting industry in Boston, MA and Providence, RI. as an announcer, news anchor, personality, interviewer, voice-over artist, and emcee. Today, Donna is a national keynote speaker and corporate communication trainer, helping companies maximize the power of their people through effective presentations and inter-

personal and remote communication. Donna is also a certified mindfulness teacher and founder of InspiringVoice.com which helps people communicate mindfully and powerfully with themselves and others. She's also the proud mother of two successful, heart-centered millennial daughters (an introvert and an extrovert) who have the great ability to communicate.

Donna's missions include fortifying future generations, and helping women and men build rich, healthy lives.

Made in the USA
Middletown, DE
03 July 2020